I Want to be Paint!

Artwork, Stories, and Poems

Colleen Kassner

I wrote *I Want to be Paint,* in 1995 and recently edited to reflect where I am today. When it was originally composed, a gallery in Milwaukee was doing an art festival in its parking lot. It was filled with artists, poets, and a collection of Milwaukee bohemians performing, displaying, and celebrating in the glorious July sun.

A long swath of paper and buckets of paint ran the length of the parking lot. It was set up for children but none were using it. That didn't last for long! Putting my bare feet in a glob of paint I proceeded to do a Cha-cha across the white paper leaving bright blue footprints in my wake. In a "Pied Piper" fashion, the children followed suit. Paint was everywhere and the peal of laughter could be heard all through the parking lot as we walked, slid, plopped and played in the paint.

Right after this it was my turn to read poetry. I sat at the edge of the stage; put my kaleidoscopic feet out in front of me, wiggled my multi-colored toes, and read.

That's when I knew I would become a painter.

I Want to be Paint

I place my passion
between oil and brush,
searching for meaning—
personhood—in visceral visions:
a face, the eyes, a Mona'ed grin.
Who is this before me
emerging from my vapored imaginings?

I can be paint.

Place me thick and glossy,
infused with aromatic linseed oil
upon this stark, barren canvas.

Give me the primary,
the primal backdrop used for
brush-strokes lifted from the palette:
vermilion, flaxen, cobalt.
Resounding passages of
impasto, layers of luminous glaze, and
nuanced light transmute into image:
a crimson detail,
a chalk-white speck,
a silent, violet shadow.

I paint.

I need no reason, no rhyme, nor verse.
I can be pigment,
be figment, be spectrum:
dreaming with eyes open,
no portrait of insanity.

This is life!

Creativity Begins

When other little girls were playing with dolls, I was drawing using crayons. The colors excited my imagination. I fantasized of someday becoming a famous designer. The teachers in grade school always called me a dreamer. But, isn't that the essence of being an artist?

I grew up and continued to dream. It took a psychiatric hospitalization for depression to release the creativity again. After the hospitalization, Philo, (then my boyfriend, now my husband), encouraged me to go into our spare room to paint. He felt it would make me feel better. A recently found picture from that time shows me sitting at the desk looking happy, with watercolors in hand and some of my very earliest works surrounding me.

Philo and I met in an artsy cafe at a "Poet's Monday" in 1994. He was cute: a poet, an artist, a photographer. My kind of a guy! We were friends at first, enjoying easy conversations about life, poetry, art, our daughters, and our youth. Our friendship evolved into a romance. We were made for each other. My family adored him; my daughter, Briana, thought he was "cool." We laughed...a lot.

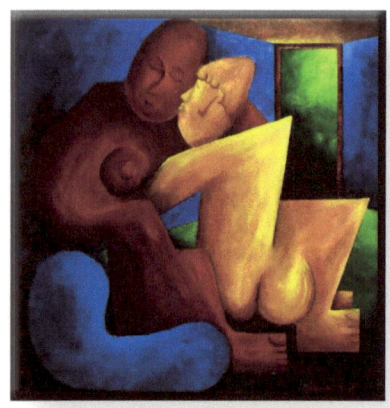

Smooch, ca. 2002
Acrylic on Canvas
24" x 24"
(Artist's collection)

While studying at the University of Wisconsin—Milwaukee to earn a degree in social welfare, my social-work internship was with a local non-profit which helped adults recover from mental illness. It was a good fit. I made Dean's List that year with a 3.8 grade point average. However, the stress and pressures started to take a toll on my stability. After not drinking for several years, alcohol re-entered the picture. Drinking was starting to interfere with my education and causing problems with my daughter and with Philo. He gave me an ultimatum: either quit or leave. Alcohol won and we broke up.

I graduated in December 1998 with a respectable grade point average. However, the years of hard work and effort seemed meaningless. I was still unstable and self-medicating with alcohol. The future looked hopeless. In the spring of 1999, I received a letter from Philo. That letter prompted the resumption of our relationship.

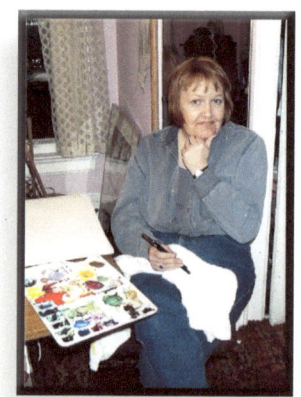

In my first studio, 2001

A Little Romance

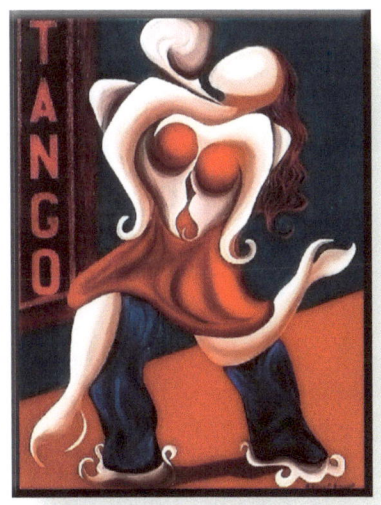

Tango, ca. 2002
Acrylic on canvas
40" x 30"
(Private collection)

Our romance rekindled. My daughter graduated from high school and was ready to be on her own. I moved in with Philo during the spring of 2000 after agreeing to quit drinking, which turned out to be difficult but not impossible. This time, I was ready. I was somewhat successful. After going for weeks without drinking, the urge for a martini would take over. I would "sneak drink," naively thinking that Philo wouldn't know. Even though this meant jeopardizing my still precarious relationship with him, I thought I could pull it off.

Between 1999 and 2001 my psychiatrist had me on an average of fourteen separate medications simultaneously. There was a shoe box filled with medications on my bedside table. There were pills for sleep, others for pain, some slowed me down and some picked me up. The medications had me revolving in and out of the psychiatric hospital every few months and in a day treatment program the rest of the time, I had become a "professional patient." Philo and I thought that this was going to be the story of our lives.

When I was in for yet another hospitalization, Philo took matters into his own hands. He looked at the boxes of medication bottles and realized that something was seriously wrong. He went to the doctor's office with me and demanded to know the purpose of each medication and why it was prescribed. The doctor didn't know. I found a new doctor. In 2001, I was put in the hospital for two weeks to titrate off all the medications and be placed on a new regimen of only two medications. Finally, I was heading in the right direction.

At this same time and more importantly, a major shift in my self-awareness was taking place. I was coming alive; the spark of my creative drive was reignited after the fog of years of over-medication had lifted. I was re-connecting with art, with the little girl drawing dolls. Spending my hospital evenings in my room with a sketch-pad I would draw for hours on end, filling page after page until I was tired enough to go to sleep. The walls of my room were covered with my drawings, some of which I still have. Art was giving me the clarity that would become the defining focus of my life.

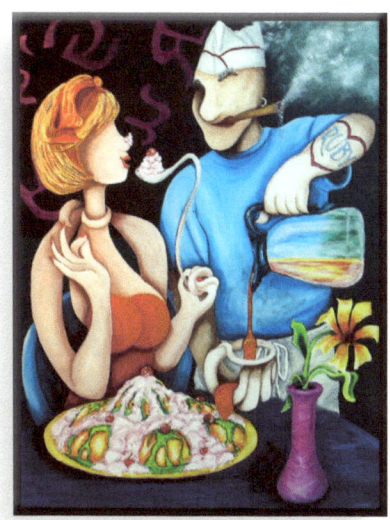

Geez Ruby, 2005
Acrylic on canvas
42" x 30"
(Private collection)

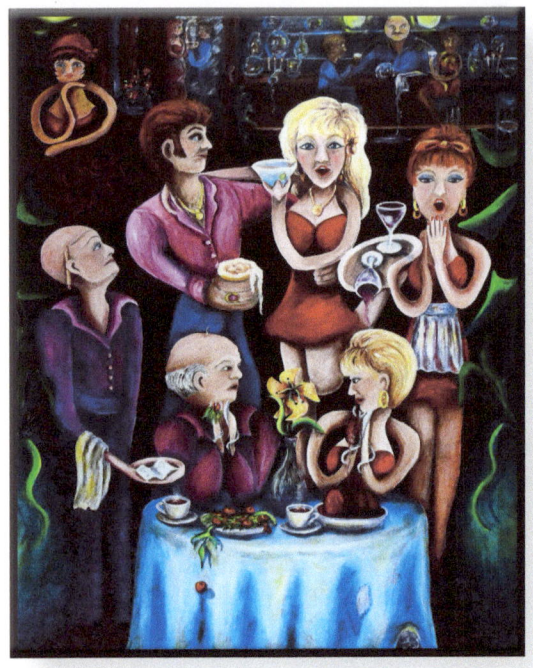

Chéz Swirl, ca. 2012
Acrylic on canvas
56" x 44"

A few days after leaving the hospital, feeling human again and slightly invincible, I thought I'd like to have a drink. So, while I was out and about, I stopped in a bistro and ordered a martini. I sipped. When I realized how stupid I was being, how much I risked losing, and just how tired I was of jeopardizing my fragile and precious stability, I set the drink down, left a generous tip, and never touched a drop again. The compulsion no longer owned me nor had power over me. I was finally free...free to recover.

After this epiphany, I began to paint in earnest. After dabbling at first with a watercolor here and a canvas there, the mood stabilizing effects of doing art began to take hold and I began to take creating art seriously. Art focused my thoughts outwardly and gave me a means of expressing myself and channeling my "manic energies" on self-affirming pursuits rather than self-annihilation.

My days were spent learning the prismatic array of techniques necessary to work with acrylics. I learned about the different qualities of pigments, how mediums worked, how to stretch a canvas, and how to layer the colors and mix them for different effects. Canvas after canvas was painted...the majority of them awful...except for *Smooch* (page 4.) I painted it on a day while Philo was at work. He came home, saw the painting. From that point forward I knew that art was going to be the focus of my life. Art—that little girl drawing dolls—was giving me my confidence back, offering me a sense of control and destiny.

In spite of all this, something was lacking. A piece of the puzzle was still missing. I loved my social worker roots and I missed helping people improve their lives. My artwork needed an expanded audience so I decided to do an art/exhibit benefit for a non-profit organization. It would reconnect me to those roots and give me a larger audience at the same time. I contacted my former internship and asked if they wanted to do something with art. The executive director was delighted and quite surprised to hear from me. She enthusiastically said, "Yes!"

We did a successful, three-day benefit in September of 2006. This event would define my future.

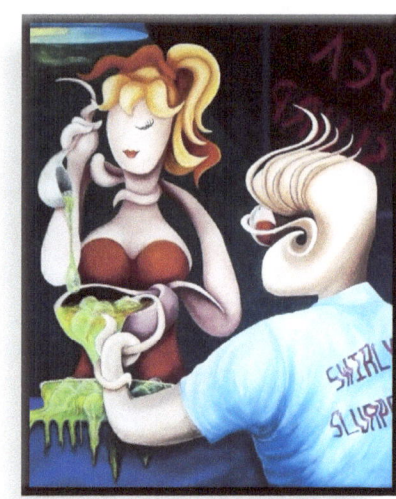

Pea Slurp, 2005
Acrylic on canvas
40" x 30"

The Invitation

I lay before you the breadth of my vulnerability,
a feast for you to savor.

The scent of life, rich with emotion
is to be consumed voraciously,
imbuing senses oblivious to reason.

Savor this Dim-Sum of emotions,
whirling in tandem, rhythmic heartbeat.
Murmur mendacity,
emptiness in my ear.

Come, sup with me.

Experience this open celebration of feminine fire.
Taste the perfume of buried emotion,
love,
sweat,
raw,
salty caviar.

Delight in delicate French Silk Pie,
skin smooth cream indulgence.

I lay before you,
open soul and flesh.
All is to share.
Drink;
deluge yourself in wine sweet desire.

Savor gently this vulnerability,
it is precious in its person,
precarious in its design.

Manic

In 2007, after the success of the benefit, I began to volunteer at the non-profit with which I was working, Grand Avenue Club (GAC.) At first it was to help out with a few creative projects. Eventually, talk ensued of a gallery for GAC. Art was becoming a popular part of GAC's many activities.

During this time I rediscovered a series of photos taken by Philo of me during my final bi-polar episode. (Most boyfriends would call a doctor...mine grabbed his camera.) The photos covered only a fifteen minute time span but expressed a myriad of emotions. The photos themselves weren't very usable. However, I sensed they would make interesting paintings. The paintings became a turning point for me, both in my art and in my mental health.

Creating these paintings, some of my earliest oils, was an intense experience. The process was visceral, causing me to relive the emotions of my mania as I worked the compositions. The paint flew onto the canvas; the images emerged as if they had a life of their own. The pain, the confusion, the exhaustion of the episode left my psyche and became the painting in front of me. I was experiencing mania again, but without the sadness, guilt, and horror of the aftermath. I was painting with a sense of clarity I had never felt before. These paintings were a symbolic farewell to my previous life of strife and chaos. They were also a beginning because they celebrated my emergence as a woman who was now capable of harnessing her own energies and creativity. They allowed me to say a final good-bye to the years that were and a warm hello to what was to become.

The *Manic* series taught me about the power of an image. We presented the works at a show in April of 2008. Many people came up to me at the opening to tell me stories of theirs, or a friend's, or a loved one's struggle with mental illness. The portraits helped them see their personal experiences through my work. The power that is within an image, the ability of a painting to reach into a person's being, is what inspired me to move forward with portraiture.

I proposed an idea to GAC's director. I would paint pictures of members. These would not be pictures of the "mentally ill" as they have sometimes been portrayed by other artists. These portraits would show the members as people with lives, with desires to belong, to be productive, and to have meaning in the world. The paintings would tell the story of their experiences with mental illness, both their triumphs and their struggles.

Images opposite page:
All are oil on canvas
30" x 40" for landscape and 40" x 30" for portrait
Top: Yellow Woman, Blue Woman
Middle: Manic, Thoughtful(in a private collection), Empty
Bottom: Done, Nasty (in a private collection), Angry

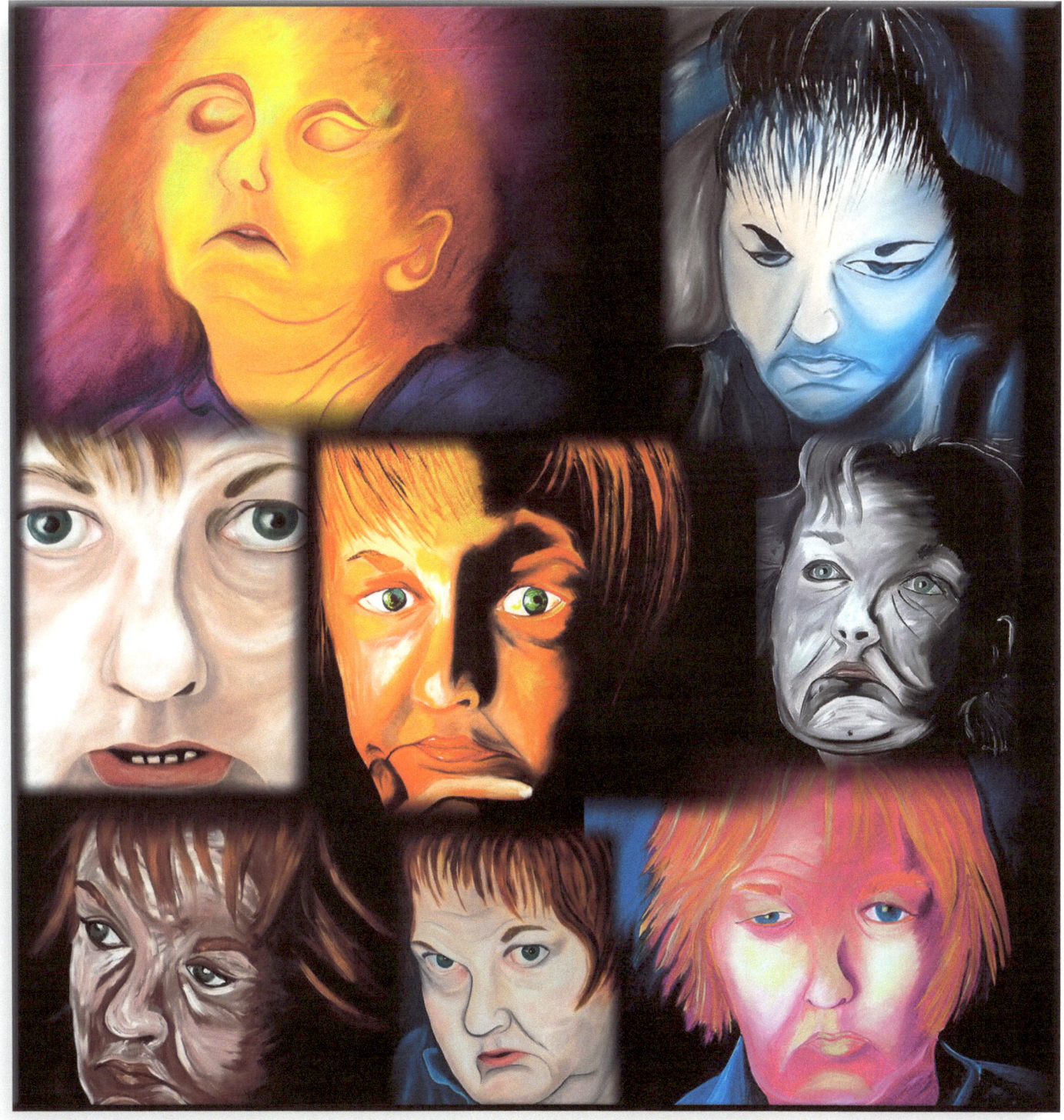

Portrait Projects

Individual Portraits

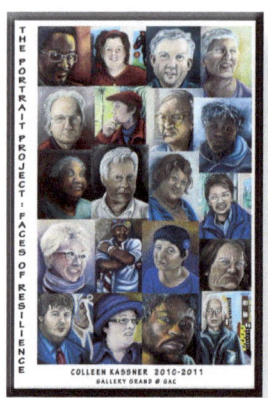

On Sunday, May 23, 2010, after having known each other for 15 years, Philo and I were married in the Gallery Grand @ GAC. We were surrounded by people who loved us and had seen us through so much. Our poet friend, Tim Kloss, performed the ceremony. Philo's family, my family, our family of friends from GAC and our wonderful artist-friends celebrated the occasion with great joy. Having the wedding in the gallery and being surrounded by so many people important to us gave the day a special significance.

In mid-June GAC was awarded, through the Greater Milwaukee Foundation, a Mary Nohl grant to fund *The Portrait Project: Faces of Resilience*. Mary Nohl was a Milwaukee, Wisconsin artist who, upon her death, left a generous endowment with the Greater Milwaukee Foundation, a portion of which funds artists working with non-profits. I felt honored to be able to work under this grant.

GAC was able to commission me to paint 15-20 portraits of its members within the course of a year. At this point my portraiture experience had been limited to a few rudimentary paintings of friends from my earlier work and the more emotional canvasses of the *Manic* series. *The Portrait Project: Faces of Resilience* was an exhilarating although daunting new challenge for me. I wanted the portraits to give voice and credence to a group of people, my friends and colleagues, who deserved recognition. So often, when living with a mental illness, a person is ignored, shunned, or trivialized. I wanted these portraits to change that.

At first, many members were shy about participating. As the project progressed the enthusiasm grew. Many of the people I chose to paint were members with whom I worked on a daily basis, some were selected because of their history with GAC, and some because I found them endearing. All of them were important; all of them had stories to tell. The biographies we collected from them to accompany the portraits were moving, empowering, and often heartbreaking. Underneath the stories, behind the paintings, were the lives of the members, people who lived with mental illness, who survived and thrived with their community.

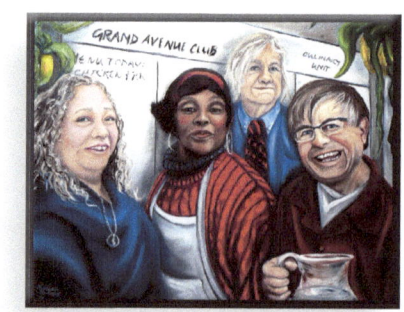

In the Cafeteria

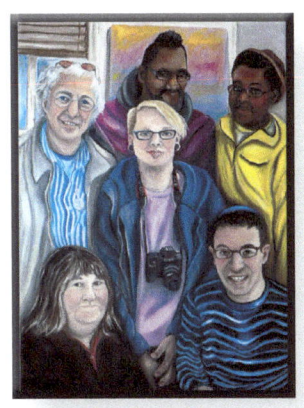

In the Gallery

This project was a monumental undertaking. I had no idea how complex and intricate creating a portrait can become. Many times, half-way through the portrait, I would hate how it looked, set it aside and start over; often several times. I was learning a lot. My perseverance with the project and my drive to complete it as best I could consumed most of my time for the entire year. My studio was filled with the canvasses of GAC members staring at me, all in various stages of completion, silently waiting to tell their story. While working on the paintings I developed an intimacy with the entire process of painting; the canvas, oils, and brushes contributed to the person I was portraying.

The Portrait Project: Faces of Resilience was difficult, rewarding, frustrating, and one of the greatest learning experiences of my life. I will be forever thankful for the opportunity to create the work that addresses such an important topic; the elimination of the stigma surrounding mental illness.

The portraits were presented at Milwaukee's Gallery Night and Day in July 2011. I then had the honor of having them grace the lobby of the Milwaukee Repertory Theater for the duration of their production of the Broadway musical, *"next to normal."* They are now housed in the reception area of GAC as part of their permanent art collection.

The Portrait Project: Faces of Resilience told a powerful story of individual recovery. However, there was much more to convey. In 2012 GAC applied for and received another Mary Nohl Grant to create four group portraits of members working within GAC. By the end of the one year grant period, six were produced. Both phases of the project were to be combined in a book written by Rachel Forman and me entitled, *Facing Forward: An Artist, a Community, and Stories of Resilience.*

Group Portraits

GAC's primary function is to give adults who have experienced mental illness the opportunity to find their way back into the world. In this phase of the project, I wanted to document the relevant work done by members at GAC by portraying them doing daily tasks. Their enthusiasm for what they do is the inspiration behind these paintings.

GAC members have important stories to tell. Some members come to GAC after many hospitalizations, years of illness, and lives in disarray, many having lost the support of family and loved ones in the process. Some are more fortunate and have family and other loved ones to assist and encourage them. They all arrive though, like my charcoal drawing on the canvas, with an outline of what is to become.

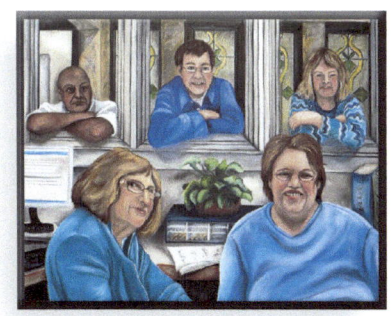

In the Office

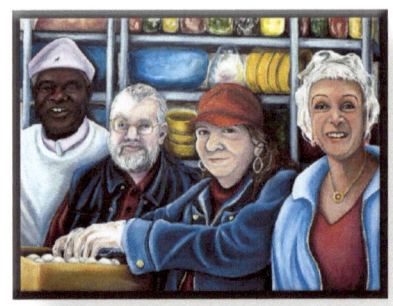

Preparing Lunch

The people I portrayed in these paintings are of different races, religions and ages. Some are young adults and others are coming into the later years of their lives. They are all vital human beings with the same needs for acceptance and success that is a part of the human condition.

The group portraits were a tremendous challenge. I had many elements to consider. There were anywhere from four to seven different people and personalities to capture. There were environments to paint, and there were many details to include. Fortunately, my skills were improving since the previous set of portraits and I was more adept at handling the difficult passages of a painting. In these compositions, I strove to capture the sense of camaraderie between members. While working in my studio, I would reflect upon what I knew about the lives of the people as I painted them. I thought a lot about what recovery is about, how the movies and news media portray images of people who deal with mental illness in a negative manner, how art had the power to alter that image, and how creating a painting aligns with the process of recovery and reintegration after mental illness.

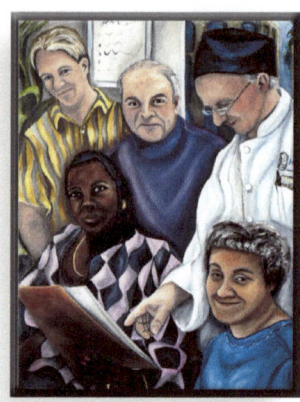

Planning Events

I created these portraits from photographic references and through personal observation of the members/subjects in their day to day lives at GAC. My technique involved using many layers of color applied in varying stages of opaqueness. I started with a charcoal outline; the shadows were added and then the figure was "fleshed out" with skin tones. During this process the image started to form and the subjects residing in the painting began to emerge and take shape.

At this nexus of creation and observation, I perceived an important parallel between recovery and the process of creating my compositions. The melding of the varying elements in a portrait is much like the blossoming of a personality during recovery. There are bumps and starts, successes and mistakes, but in the end, the picture is completed. After the elements have all been put in place the portrait—the person—is complete.

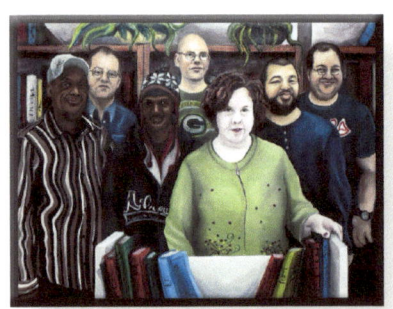

In the Library

In all, I painted 51 people in the portraits, 20 in the individual portraits and 31 in the groups. The first phase of the project tells the narrative of the individual; the second phase reveals the people of a community and their relationships. The project in both phases humbled me, made me mature as an artist, and allowed me to leave behind, long after I am dust, the stories of the people who have touched my life so deeply.

The paintings in the Individual Portraits are 30" x 24" or 24" x 30" landscape and portrait
The Group Portraits are all 30" x 40" or 40" x 30" landscape and portrait
All paintings are oil on canvas

Louise

She was a woman who could change personalities
like some women change clothes.
She stood at the edge
of a minute
tapping out time to the tune of the
"Thorazine Shuffle."

She changed clothes like some women
change personalities.
She was a living cornucopia of voices and hallucinations,
drowning in confetti cups
of psychoactive pill-pops.

She'd down her confetti
like most women down chocolate,
tucking away tidbits twixt
bra and breast
stockpiling her evening cocktail.
(A sweet mix of Clozaril, Deseryl, Mellaril.)

She'd test her edge,
teetering between raging delusions
or tumbling into a
PDR-with-a-shot-of-vodka-supper-time-sleep.

She was a woman who changed emotion
like some women change their minds.
When she was lucid, she was very, very lucid
but
when she fell from the edge
she'd splash into the lunacy ball.

She said one day, "I'm thirty five years old!
I didn't know it wasn't normal to hear voices.
NO ONE EVER TOLD ME!

The world stopped, frozen at the edge of a minute.
This is all you get, the voices whispered.

This...Is...All...You...Get...

Chelsea Hotel

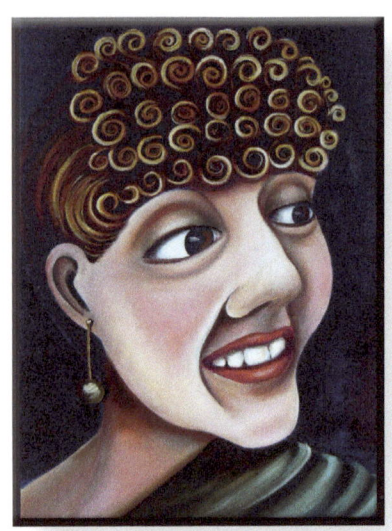

Chelsea Belle
Ca. 2008/9
Oil on canvas
30" x 24"
(Private collection)

Philo took me to stay at the iconic Chelsea Hotel in Manhattan on a dare. I had only been to New York for brief periods in 1969 and 1972. This was 2004 and things had changed drastically since those years...except for the Chelsea Hotel. The hotel had a rich history of artists and bohemians who graced its halls and rooms. We stayed there for four consecutive vacations until the hotel was sold. After the sale, most of the colorful artists and people were either evicted or moved out. Now, it is being converted to a "boutique" hotel.

When we arrived at the Chelsea, I was agog at the funkiness of the hotel. To say it was colorful is an understatement. We checked in and settled into our shabby, chrome-yellow painted room, with nails in the walls for our clothing, tattered drapes, a lumpy and quite squeaky mattress, and threadbare carpet. We awoke early the next morning and ventured down to the lobby. The late night revelers were returning home.

Upon entering the lobby, we were greeted by a drag queen sauntering in from her night's performance, sans wig and in full make-up, a peacock colored, sequined mini dress, and six inch stilettos—replete with fish-net stockings.

Who needs Broadway when you have the lobby of the Chelsea Hotel?

Artists also loved and lived in the Chelsea. In the center of the hotel was a 10 story iron-balustrade staircase that was lined top to bottom with paintings collected in lieu of back-rent. We would take the elevator up to the 10th floor then walk the staircase down to the lobby. The halls echoed with our footsteps as the ghosts and history of past tenants followed us down the stairs.

The lobby was the main-stage of the Chelsea. The artists, residents, and many guests would congregate there to people watch, chat, and see–and–be–seen. One artist in particular, the "Artiste" as we called him, would set up his easel in the lobby, sketch books at his side, and squint carefully at his canvas as he "worked." It was quite a show. However, I later noticed that the whole time he was at his canvas there was never any paint on his brush. A different artist would wait until he saw a guest in the lobby and then pull out his cell phone and proceed to call his "agent" about his latest art deal. He would be mid-conversation about the megabucks he was making on the deal, and if the hotel guest would get up to leave, he would snap the phone shut until the next person would arrive and the performance would start again—it's the audience that counts at the Chelsea!

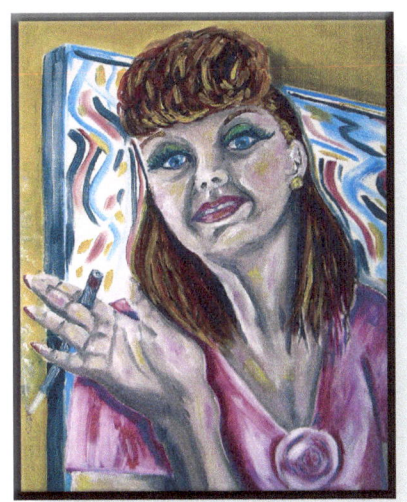

Cha-Cha LaRoux
Ca. 2009
Oil on canvas
30" x 24"

Some of the stories at the Chelsea are funny and some poignantly sad. There was a woman, we called her the "Teacher," who would sit in the lobby for hours reading to an imaginary class of children from the imaginary book in her hand. She was quite animated while reading and I'm sure, to her, the children were very real.

A year later, when we returned to the Chelsea, Philo and I had a room next to hers. Ours, though shabby, was clean with a bed and sheets. In hers was a soiled and bare mattress on a cot. The nicotine stains and odor permeated the decor of broken blinds, peeling paint, and dirt encrusted windows. The following year when we stayed at the Chelsea, she was gone.

Philo and I genuinely loved the Chelsea Hotel and dearly miss the chaotic entertainment of its lobby and its plethora of interesting and quirky tenants. Our stays there stimulated this series of paintings. Although there are only a few they are based either on real people or composites of people we would see while relaxing in the ever-changing lobby. Chelsea Belle is a whimsical interpretation of the women we would see in the hotel. Cha-Cha La-Roux is totally fictional. However, I have decided that she was a down-and-out "Rockette" living out the rest of her years in a one room apartment in the Chelsea Hotel—something that is a real possibility.

Stormé DeLarverie

At one of our stays, whilst whiling away the afternoon in the world's best lobby, we saw her. We called her the "Pshew" lady. As we were watching the assorted characters meander in and out, we saw an old woman who bedraggled but determined leave the hotel. She had on well-worn army boots, a tattered denim shirt, and a denim hat that had seen better days. We didn't think much of it. We saw her all the time. A few hours later, the woman came through the front door of the hotel in the weaving dance step of inebriation. We could see her eyes aiming for the elevator located at the far end of the lobby. Her focus was intense as she navigated the obstacle course of hotel furniture, area rugs, suitcases and planters that seemed to jump in front of her as she zigzagged through the lobby. Her dance was well timed and when she arrived at the reception desk she let out an audible, "Pshew!"

One of the residents yelled out, "Hello, Stormé."

That was our introduction to one of the most interesting people we met at the Chelsea. Stormé DeLarverie was a well-loved, long term resident of the hotel. She had lived there for nearly 40 years when we met her. Her colorful past was not obvious, but, one evening she shared her amazing history with us. Stormé had been the drag-king emcee in the drag-queen extravaganza, *The Jewel Box Review*. In the 1950's and 60's she traveled throughout the United States and Europe with the *Review*. She was of mixed race and, often in the US, had to "pass" in order to get into the venues. At 89 years old, she still "packed heat." She was once the body-guard for the photographer Diane Arbus's children. She is purported to be the person who threw the first punch at the 1969 Stonewall Inn Riots in Greenwich Village. Her presence there is credited, either through lore or fact, with launching the gay rights movement. She was a pioneer in the movement and well respected by the LGBT community.

She died in a nursing home in Brooklyn on May 24, 2014 at the age of 94. I am happy to have had the privilege of knowing her and creating a portrait of her that confers respect and dignity to such an interesting person.

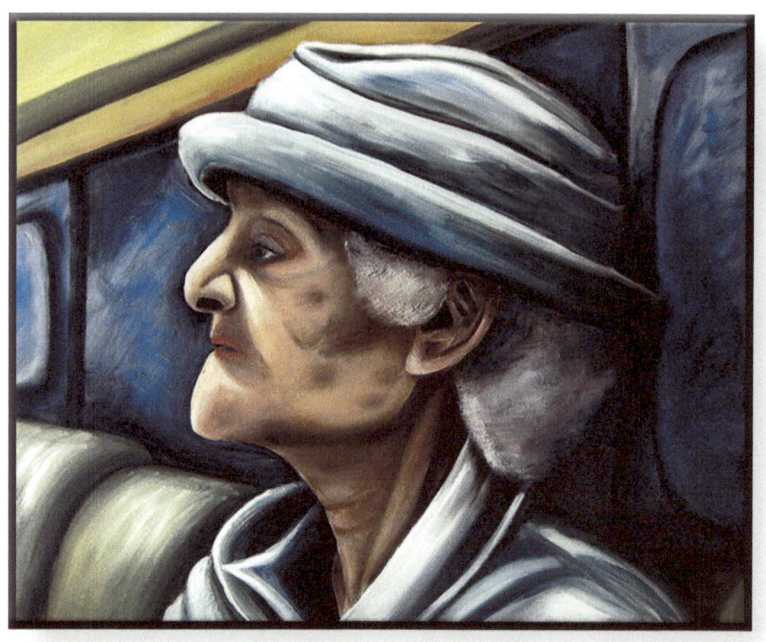

Stormé DeLarverie, ca. 2009
Oil on canvas
24" x 30"
(Private collection)

Blue Women

The *Blue Women* series was created after I returned home from another psychiatric hospitalization. I had uncontrolled and undiagnosed diabetes. It took an astute nurse to find the problem. I vowed then to never have another psychiatric hospitalization—one I have kept.

Psychiatry, is the first painting of this series. It was born late one night, when I woke crying in frustration from the trauma of the hospitalization. Philo told me to go into the studio and "paint it out." A blank canvas was already on the easel so I grabbed a brush full of red paint and painted the stripes on the canvas, yellow was applied to the background, and then purple was applied for the mountains. An intense blue was selected for the figure that is seen ripping aside the mountains to climb through and surmount them. I see this painting as an allegory of my hospital experience.

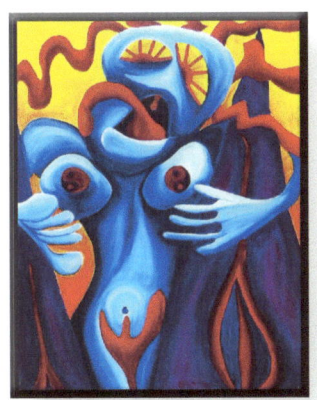

Psychiatry, ca. 2003
Acrylic on canvas
42" x 30"

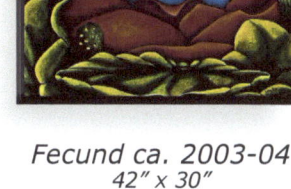

Fecund ca. 2003-04
42" x 30"
Acrylic on canvas

Blue Women has become the genre that speaks to my interpretations of feminine power and strength. The pieces have matured through time. Included in this book are six paintings representing the evolution of the series.

The painting, *Fecund*, (upper right) is the last painting of this series that is done in acrylic. The seated figure is nestled in a lotus and embraces a seed pod ripe with fertility. It was painted after experiencing several years of stability and expressed my artistic emergence. Soon after completing this work I switched to oil paints. The first Blue Woman done in this medium is *Contemplation*. She is an abstracted figure resting in a garden of calla lilies, calm and reposed in thought. She was completed during a time when I was wondering about where my work would be heading and what lied ahead for my art.

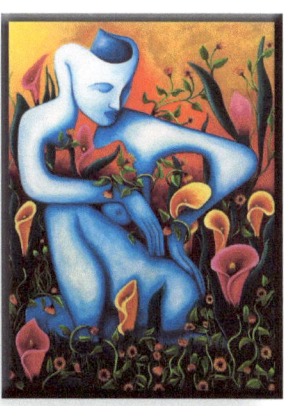

Contemplation 2007
Acrylic on canvas
48" x 36"

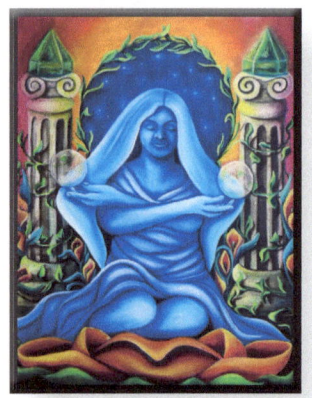

Balance, 2012
Oil on canvas
48" x 36"

The next two paintings in the series, *Wisdom* and *Balance* express the continuation of my emotional experiences. I had reached a point of *Wisdom*—self-confidence so-to-speak—in my work and now felt that I wanted to give to others because of my recovery. It is *Balance* that conveys the delicate symbiosis of my sense responsibility to others and my art. It is a balance as precarious as the bubbles that rest upon her fingertips.

With my most recent addition to the series, *Strength*, I envisioned a woman arising from an inferno and coming into the light. In the painting she has chains binding her to the burning earth beneath, yet, in her grasp they become flowered vines. She triumphs. She has climbed from the depths of hell into the light. It portrays what I know to be true. That a woman has great power, she can overcome many obstacles, she is beautiful in her own right, and can carry this light and beauty to others.

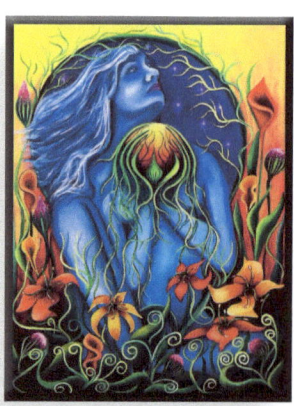

Wisdom, 2011
Oil on canvas
48" x 36"

The images in the Blue Woman series were born from a very painful time. Their evolution in both style and medium reflect my journey from beginning artist, to one discovering her way, to the artist I am today. The journey has been a long one. Where it will head from here? That is unknown. I do know this; the series will continue to grow and evolve just as I will as a human being. This is the most amazing part of life. It's always growing and always changing.

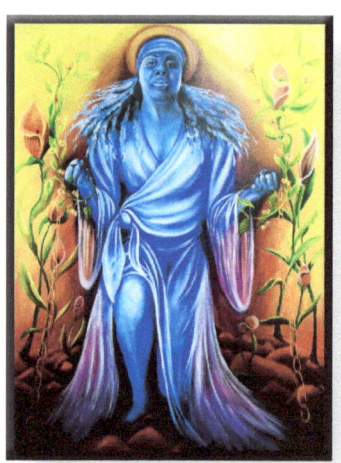

Strength, 2015
Oil on canvas
48" x 36
(Private collection)

Black Orchid

I am the diaphanous woman of dawn's lavender mist.
A mystical, veiled countenance; wandering,
questioning, seeking ephemeral wisdom.

I rise as the sun, into conscious configuration
condensed from vaporous mist into
Occidental Goddess guiding self forward.

In the naked yellow day
I become a gypsy at the carnival,
hawking trinkets of pretense,
fool's gold for the psyche.
I am not of this life nor life past
nor life to come.

I am the gypsy, amorphous soul,
seeking lemniscate crown
in trade for false trinkets unsold.
I realize upon noon that
omniscience is not purchased, but earned.

I transmute into evening's black-orchid-panther;
a sleek sensuous cat,
stalking the labyrinth of feline fecundity,
pregnant with seeds of courage.

As the black-orchid night prowler,
I become stronger, wiser, swifter, timeless.
I possess eyes that glow with the golden knowledge of the crone.
I can suckle my infants, protect my territory,
purr with sexuality, and roar with rage.

I return from the labyrinth
and curl into my cat body sated with wisdom and incisive power,
sleeping within my womanhood, until I am, again,
the diaphanous lavender dawn.

Wise Women

Womanhood—the lives of women, the emotions of women, and the strength of women—is a continuing theme in my painting. We are a remarkable gender. We are mothers, daughters, sisters, wives, lovers, and partners, keepers of the home and leaders of nations. We can laugh at ourselves, cry for another, and we endure.

My coming of age years were in the mid-1960—70's. *Women's Lib* was a new movement. The women leading the way were iconic. Gloria Steinem, Betty Friedan, Angela Davis broke open the dam of female power and pride. We are still fighting the battles. The fight is long, difficult, but I believe we will succeed.

Today we are a global community. Technology has made communication instantaneous. I can hold a world of information in the palm of my hand. This globalism makes one acutely aware of the plight of people throughout the world. More than 50% of those people are women, a good portion of whom cannot or are not allowed to enjoy the freedoms I take for granted. I am now conscious of a world in which women are shrouded, mutilated, discriminated against, and still considered the property of a man. Often, it leaves me feeling helpless.

We need now, in this day and this world, to bond together as a gender—as humans—to become a bastion of support, leadership, and hope for our next generations. I am hopeful that this new generation soon will discover leaders as strong, as vocal, and as persistent as the women who influenced and led my youth.

The art I create may seem small when compared to the scope of the world's problems. It is, however, not insignificant. It is an interpretation of my world that is shared with others. If it can speak to the "humane-ness" of people, if it can tell stories of courage and hope, if it touches some chord within the viewer's psyche, I am happy. I have done my job.

Della

Della is the first portrait in the Wise Women series. The series originally was going to be called, Water Women, but it evolved as it went along. When I called Della about being in a portrait for this series, I asked whether it would be acceptable to show her holding water. She said, "Of course! I'm a Pisces!"

Della is portrayed in my backyard on a sunny July afternoon. The violet flowers, astrological glyphs, and water were incorporated to honor her Piscean nature.

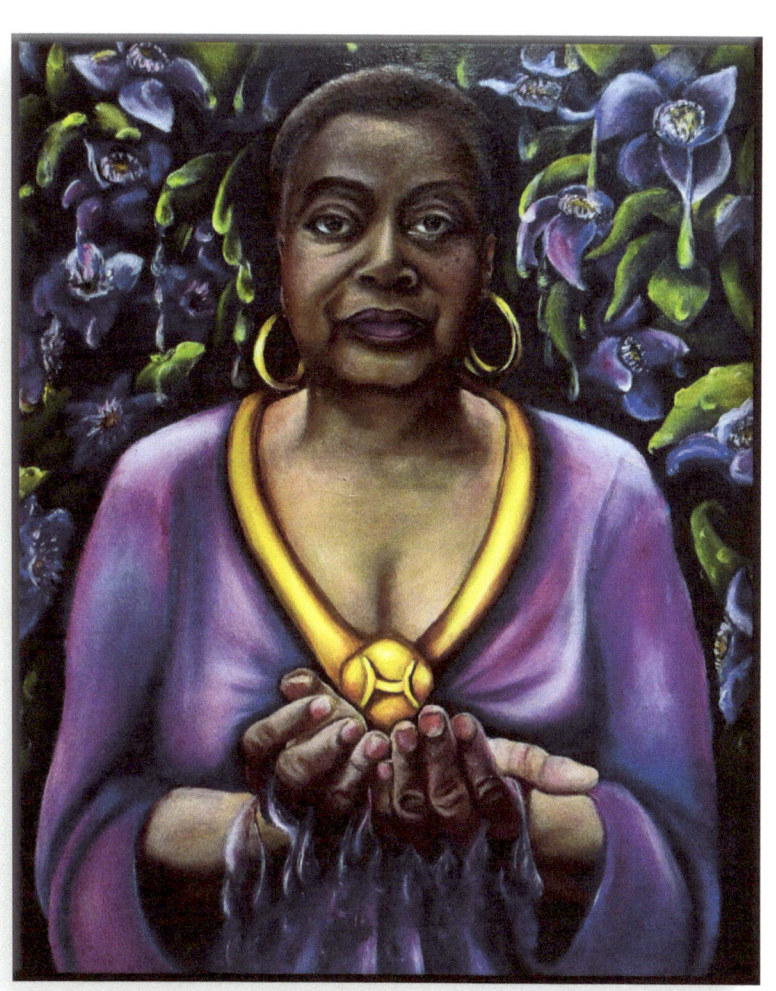

2014
Oil on canvas
30"x 24"

Debra

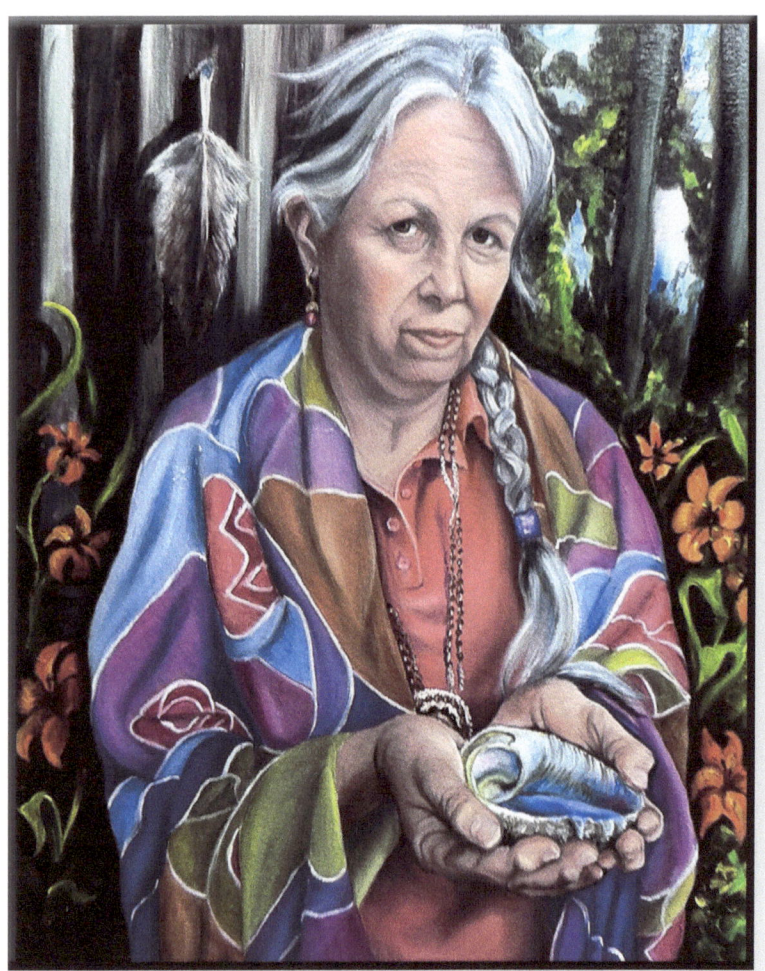

Deb is one in our group of eclectic artists who meet on Friday nights. Together we discuss life, art, other artists, the art scene, Hollywood gossip, music, politics, and our lives. As a cozy circle of kindred spirits, we can laugh, share our woes and successes, and be with friends. We call it our "Prayer Meeting."

She is the second woman in the series. The late July summer was lush and verdant at this point. I captured her during the mid–afternoon sun, again in our backyard. As a Native American, she holds the traditions of her culture dearly. She is presenting a shell she uses in her Native ceremonies. In the background hangs an eagle feather, a sacred symbol for her Oneida tribe.

2014
Oil on canvas
30"x 24"

Susie

It's hard to say "Susie" without saying "Susie and Harvey." They are an inseparable and delightful couple. They share many of the same interests that Philo and I do and have been our good friends for a long time. We do have our differences. They love forests, foraging, and nature; Philo and I love skyscrapers, neon, and concrete.

In early August, the summer was already waning. She was surrounded by the trees in our backyard. A beam of sunlight broke through the trees and illuminated her face, leaving the rest of her in lovely blue-green shadows. It is the lighting of a portraitist's dream.

She is holding paint brushes hand-made by Harvey. It is a lovely touch that seems to connect her to him through the painting.

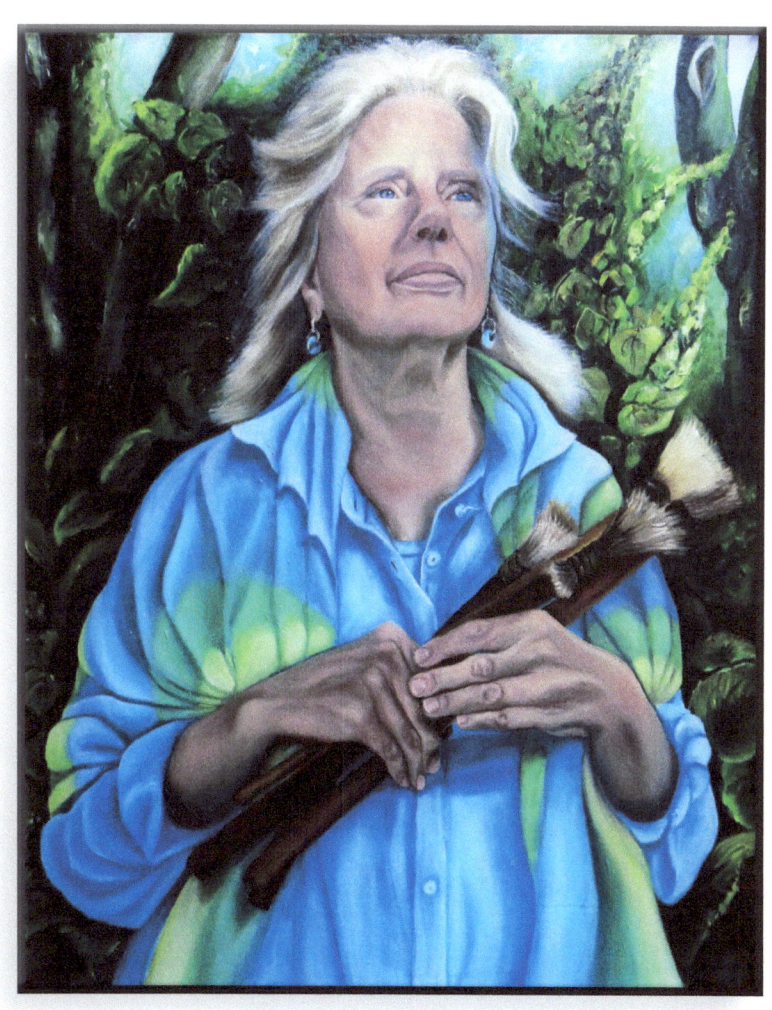

2014
Oil on canvas
30"x 24"

Carol

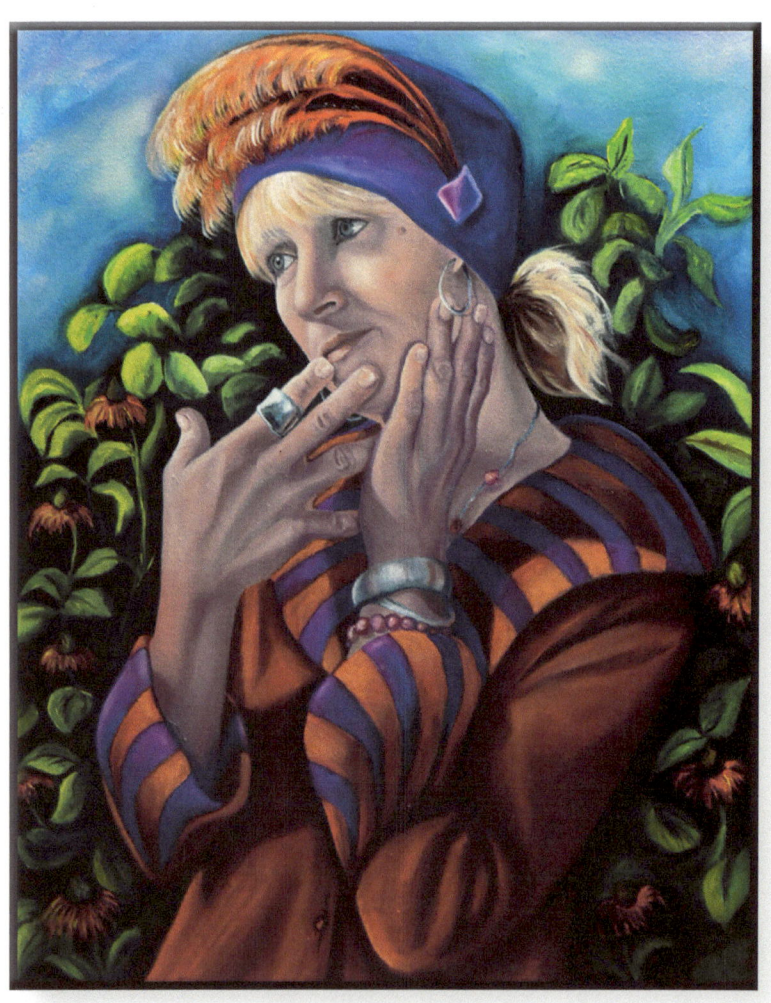

When I asked Carol to model for this series, I stated that it was to be called the "Wise Women." But, for her portrait only, I would rename it the "Wise Women and the Wise-assed Woman." It was said in loving jest and Carol thought it was an apt title.

However, I sense Carol is far more complex and has many layers to her persona. She is a fabulous pastel artist, doing edgy portraits of women, often reflecting her inner realm; a place deep and unknown to many but alluded to through her artwork. She is also the fiercely proud mother of two young adults who beautifully reflect her personality.

2014
Oil on canvas
30"x 24"

Briana

Briana, my daughter, has grown into a lovely young woman and is a talented photographer. She is a woman who is independent, self-assured, kind, just, hardworking, beautiful and creative.

Autumn is a beautiful season and Briana's favorite. It is with pride and undying love that I created this painting. Capturing the light in Briana's eyes, the glow in her skin tones, and her lovely smile are my gift to her. I hope this love is evident in the painting and that it remains in her heart and life long after I am gone.

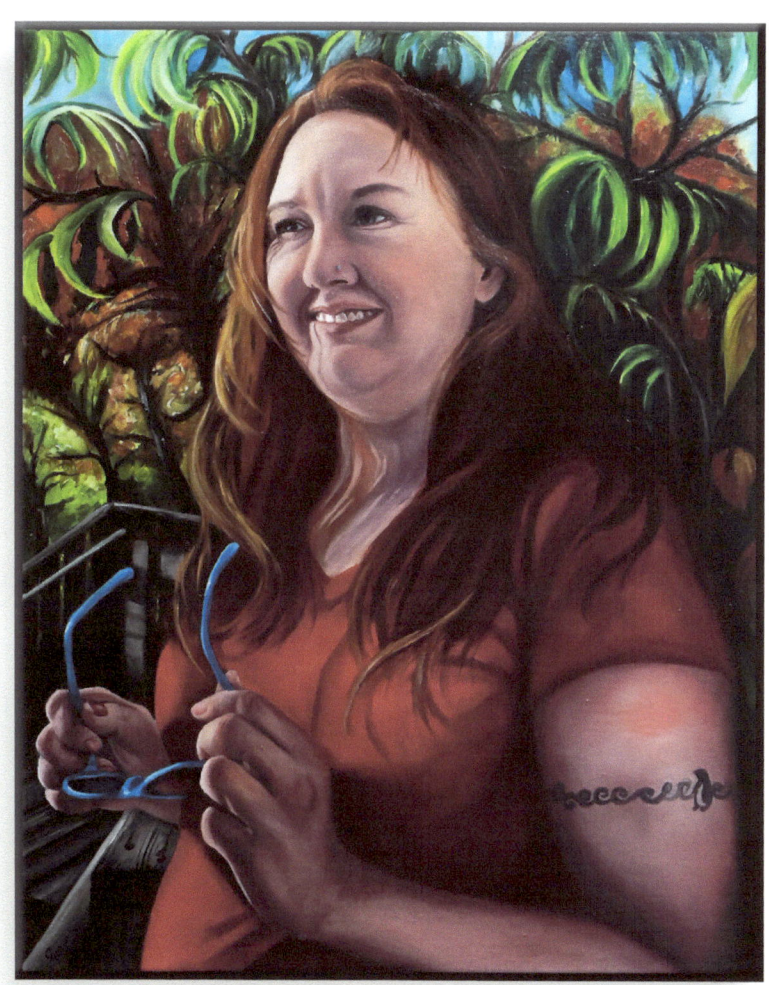

2015
Oil on canvas
30"x 24"

Stonie

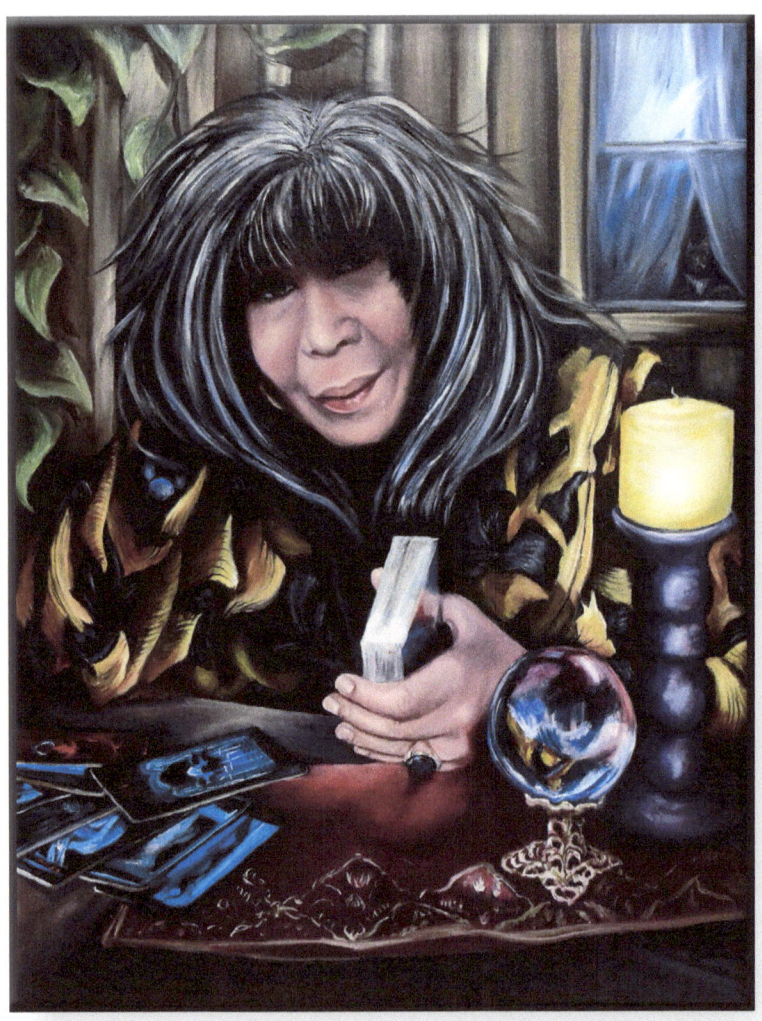

2015
Oil on canvas
30"x 24"

There are many words to describe Stonie Rivera: a woman of substance, mother, grandmother, punk rock musician, song writer, nurse, activist, artist, gallerist, world traveler, wife, psychic, author, and most of all, friend.

I met Stonie at her Dominion Gallery which she ran with aplomb and a verve that was a joy to experience. We became instant friends. We found out a lot of our philosophies were the same. We were both active in advocating for mental health, she as a former psychiatric nurse, me as a social worker. Alas, the progression of gentrification forced her to close her gallery but we both are still active in the arts community.

It was mid–September in this painting and the sun was thinning in the western sky. Stonie set up her crystal ball, her Tarot cards and candle, and the portrait was born.

Artist as Subject

My creative years began as a writer. Lesson number one was: write what you know. That lesson is carried forward into my painting. I paint who and what is familiar; the beauty in lives of fellow artists, bohemians, and eccentrics. Whether painters, photographers, musicians, or appreciators of such, capturing what is underneath the social exterior is my goal. Sometimes the person is portrayed in a humorous vein, sometimes seriously, and sometimes as a person of deep beauty, whether male or female. Portraiture is one of my modes of creation. It records for history the image of a person in a manner that is time honored.

The other lesson as a writer was, "Create mood and environment." My newest work, 'The Ghosts of Goldmann's', transfers my literary lessons to the visual realm. Assembled in the painting are a rag-tag collection of friends and associates at the remnants of the lunch counter from Goldmann's Department Store on Mitchel Street. The store dates back into the 1930's and remained a family business until its closure in 2007.

In December of 2015, it was casually mentioned by a friend that the original lunch counter was housed in a Milwaukee warehouse. My jaw dropped, my eyes widened and I immediately knew that it had to be painted. An inquiry was made to the owner of the warehouse to see if I could do a photo shoot at the lunch counter. Happily, he approved. A crew of friends, my daughter, her boyfriend, and my husband descended upon the warehouse to produce the reference photos. Although much of the original layout of the lunch counter was gone, the essence remained and is captured in this painting. Replicating the original diner on this 3 by 5 foot canvas wasn't the goal. I sought to create the image of a memory...of a time long passed and dearly loved.

The other portraits in this section follow both rules. I painted people I knew in familiar and/or created environments. The styles of portraits are personalized to the individual. Some saw themselves as opera characters, some are portrayed within their personal environments, and some left the interpretation up to me. Regardless of the back-story or my motives behind choosing a particular person, the portraits became a personal exploration of a fellow artist.

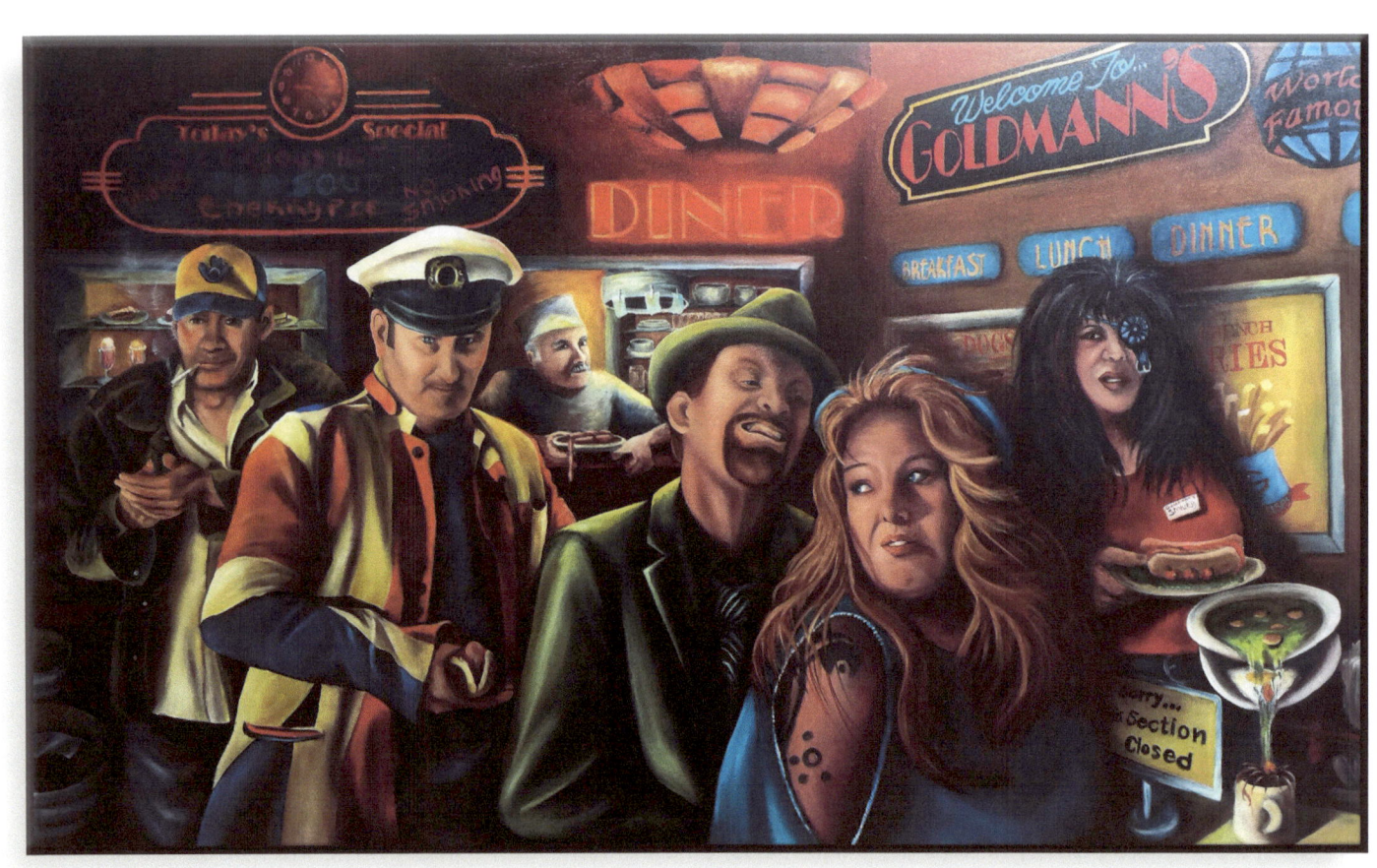

The Ghosts of Goldmann's
Oil on canvas
36" x 60"
2016

Coffee House

We sip conversation, gulp laughter like August's lemonade,
and ponder the quilts of human diversity as we sit
tabled near the frost canvased windows,
witnessing the entering and exiting of time.
Wells of thought revolve and evolve
from profound to inane as doors slam
onto Reality Street.

Winter slops brown-sugar slush on the "street demons"
as the Mercedes clad mystic parks,
praying to stay clean.
The frigid ones watch,
return to corners unseen,
their hidden lives,
clammy confusion.

Another java crashes the illusion
of existential intellectualization
as to what should be done.
Oh, Hell! We decide to go through
the door just for fun.

They mystic was right.

There's nothing clean in Reality Street's glow
when we have little and they have none.
It pisses us off 'cause it spoiled the fun,
as caffeine rush fades and empathy fails to cure.

We return to brimming ash trays and
barren cups knowing
it's just a typical Friday night.

Don Giovanni Wannabe

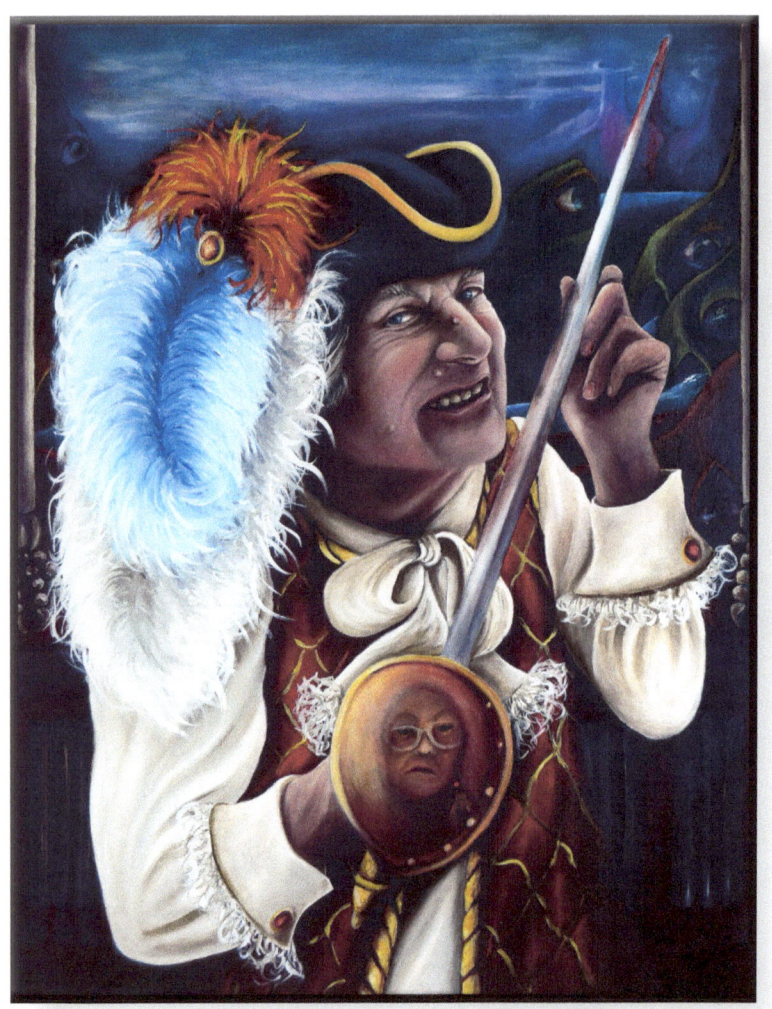

2015-16
Oil on panel
30" x 24"

Francis (Frank) Ford was the first artist I approached for this series of portraits. Not only is Frank a world class portrait photographer he is also an avid lover of opera.

When I asked Frank if he could be any character, real or fiction, without a moment's hesitation, he chose "Don Giovanni." Costumes were rented, photos were taken, and research was done.

Ergo, the painting.

China Allure

Ingrid Eubanks, also known as China Artist, was a model in an fashion-as-art show Stonie Rivera and I curated. At the fitting, Ingrid was trying on different ensembles and the designer wrapped her hair in a golden lamé headdress. The stage lights reflected off of the satiny fabric creating a prism of colors encircling her face. The make up, sparkles and palliates, was added for drama. The painting needed no background. The model held the work on her own.

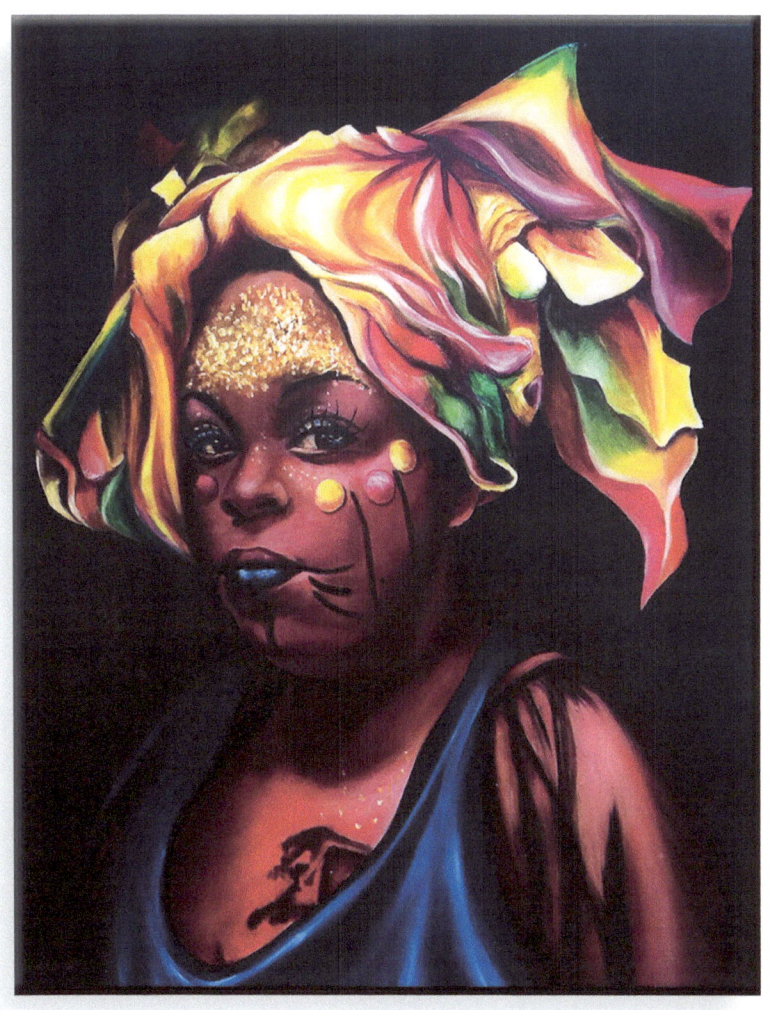

2016
Oil on panel
30" x 24"

The Table is Turned

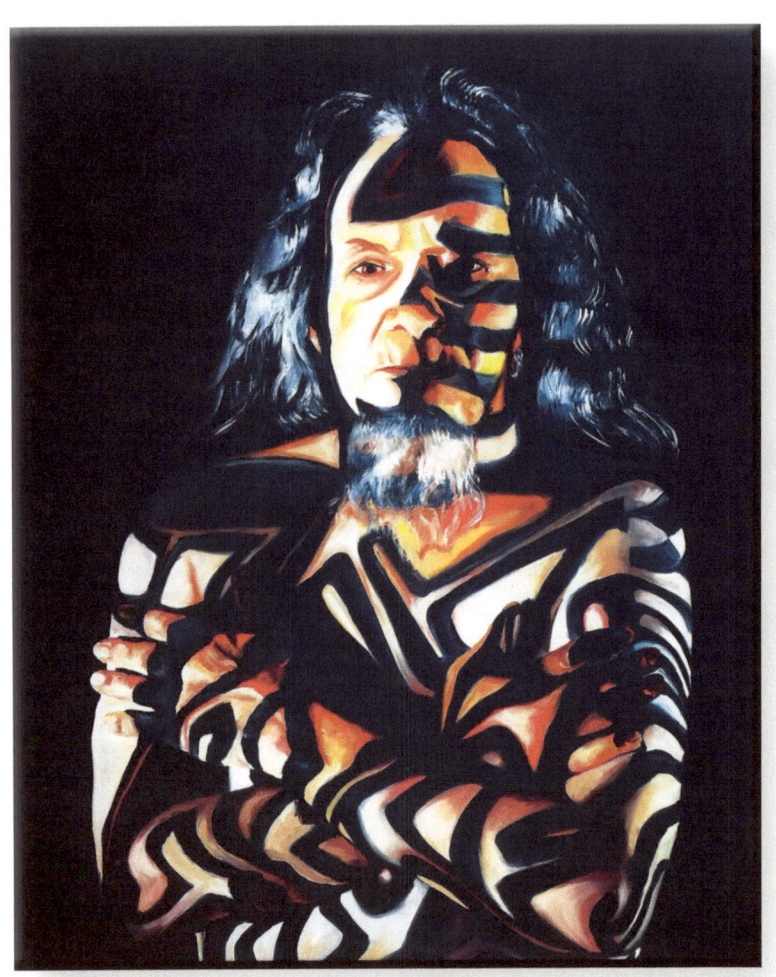

Michael R. Flasch is a renowned fine art photographer and image maker. His work is composed of the female nude posed with patterns embracing her form. He now takes the forms and combines them into complex and intriguing montages.

When I approached about doing this painting he became very self conscious about posing. It is much harder being on the other side of a lens.

2016
Oil on panel
30" x 24"

Bill and His Creepy Dolls

William (Bill) Zuback's photography is comprised of nude portraiture. His work has an otherworldly aura to it. He searches for the theme of identity and individuality within his portraiture. He is a quiet and serious man with a penchant for collecting "creepy dolls."

I had this image in mind well before I contacted Bill to take the reference photos. The color scheme evolved as the painting developed.

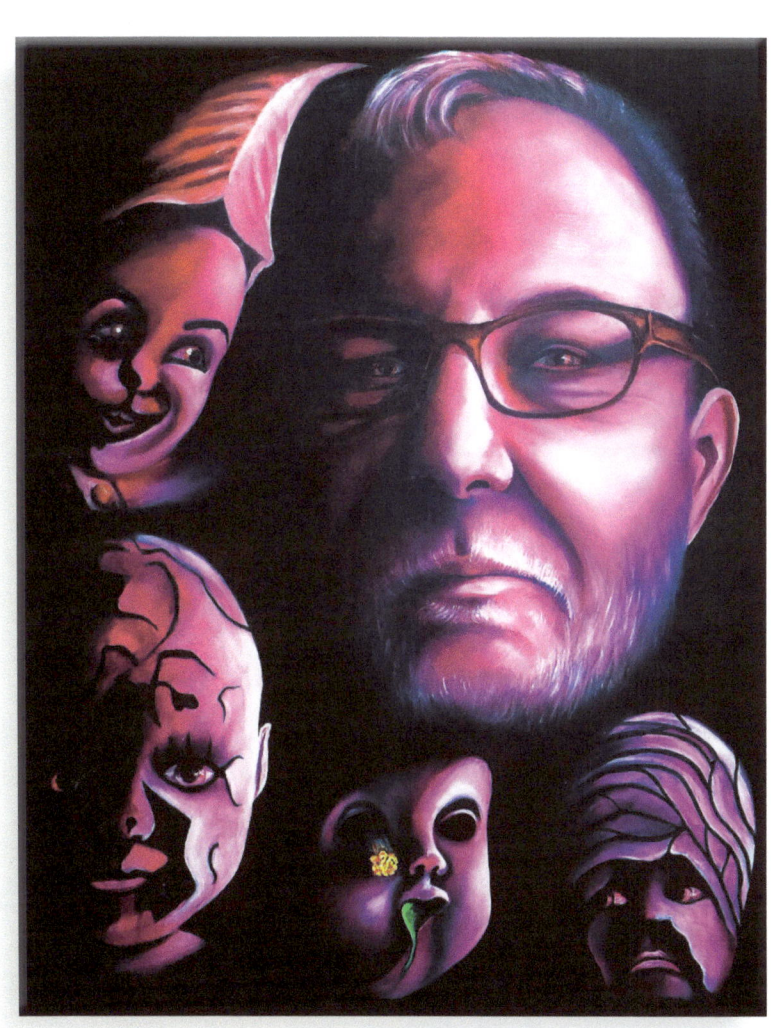

2016
Oil on panel
30" x 24"

Baubles, Bangles, and Beads

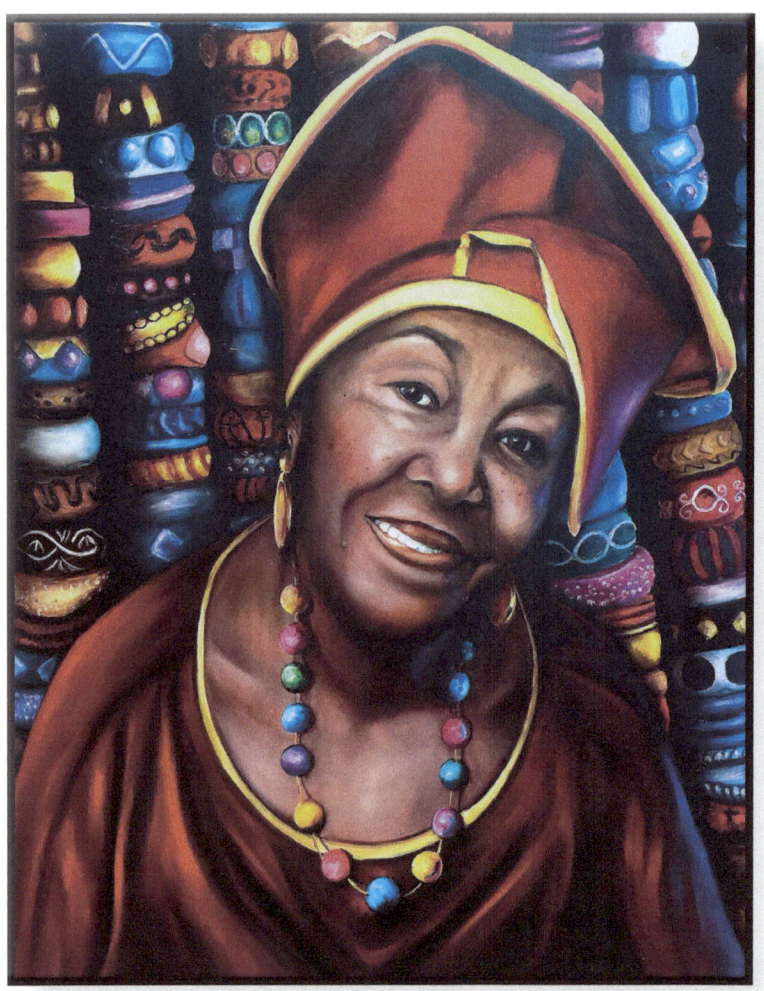

2016
Oil on panel
30" x 24"
(Private collection)

Rosemary Ollison is the most energetic and prolific folk artist I have ever known. Her work is filled with color and personality. Her creativity, according to Rosemary, "Is a gift from Jehovah, God." He is indeed generous with Rosemary!

Her small apartment is filled with testament to her artistry. For this painting she was seated in front of the bangles she likes to acquire. They are held on wooden dowels about five feet tall. There are hundreds of them and they are one of her favorite collections. It was a joy to capture her warm nature and her colorful bangles in this painting.

Madonna of the Oriental Theater

Jeanne Marie Spicuzza is a woman of multiple talents. I first knew her from the poetry scene in Milwaukee. She is a gifted poet and can cast a spell upon an audience with her fiery words.

We lost contact. Unbeknownst to me, she had moved to Los Angeles to make independent films. She succeeded.

Her first full length independent film, "The Scarapist" premiered and the Oriental Theater in Milwaukee. The Oriental is a historic landmark and the movie house carries all the features and charms of the early days of Hollywood. Jeanne asked Philo and me to photograph the premiere. I was only interested in capturing her natural beauty in this elegant surrounding.

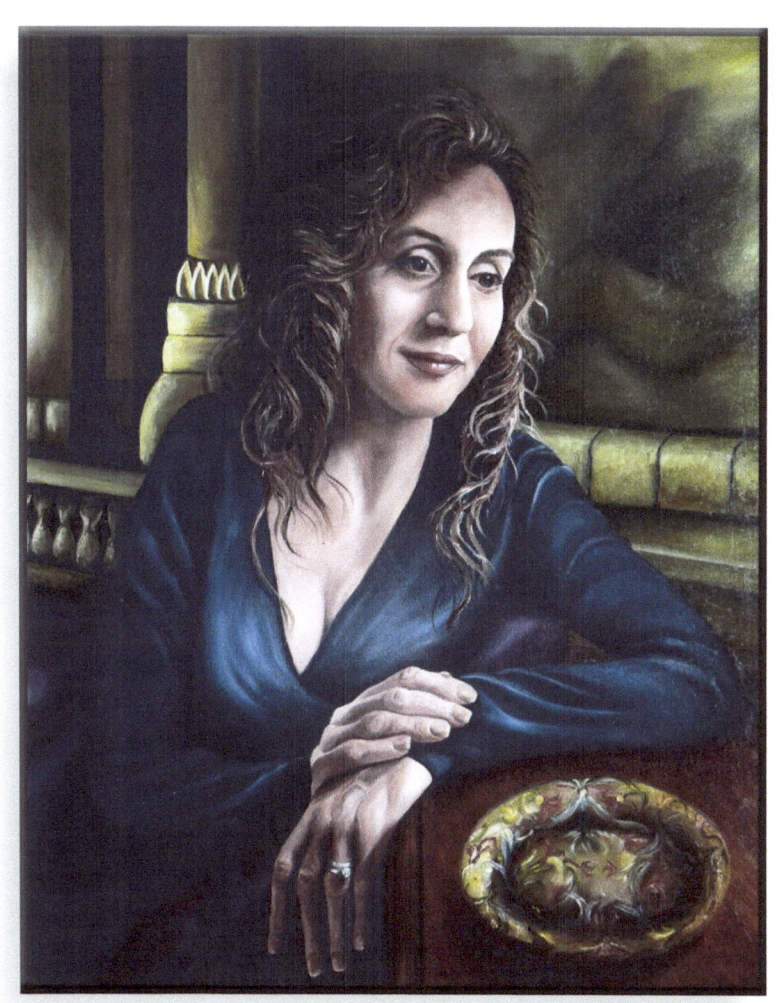

2016
Oil on panel
30" x 24"

Harvey and his Beloved Trumpet

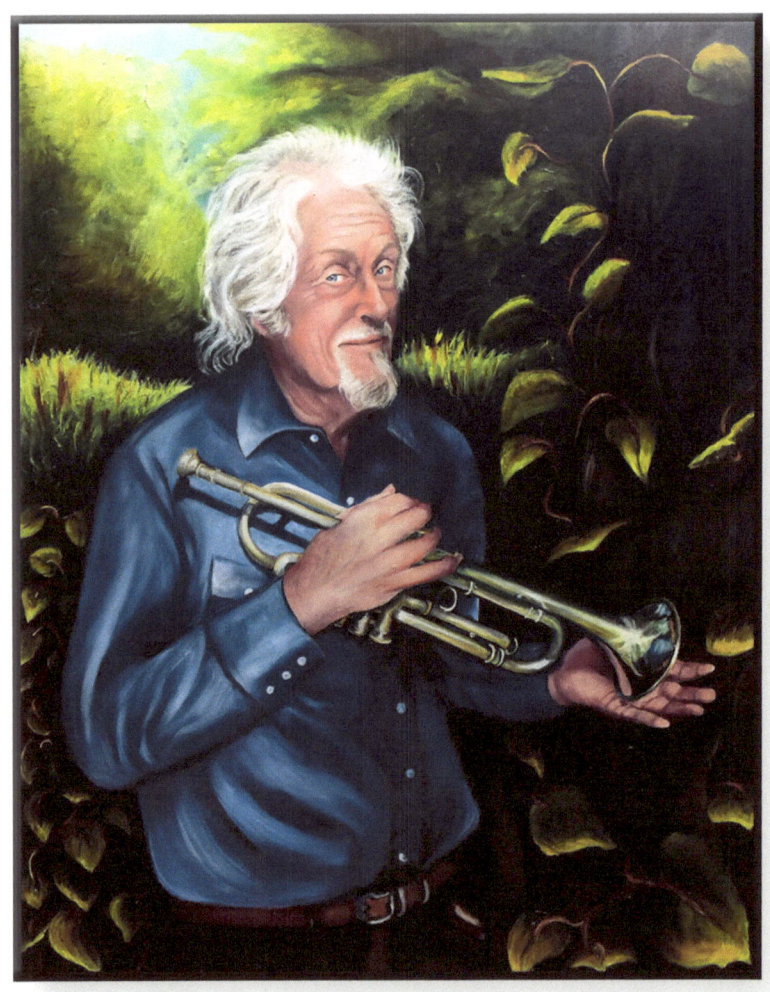

Harvey Taylor, Susie Krause's loving partner, is an institution of Milwaukee activism, music, and poetry. He has worked closely with me on several gallery shows I curated. His music and words were an enthusiastic addition to the artwork displayed in the shows. His love of life and nature exudes from his personality. He is a fine gentleman and kind soul.

2016
Oil on panel
30" x 24"

Milwaukee Blacksmith

Kent "The Colonel" Knapp is a hard working blacksmith. It is a lost art and there a few left producing. Although horseshoes are no longer a necessity, he creates customized iron work for historic preservation, homeowners, and public spaces.

His company is family run and he, his wife, four older children work loyally and diligently to keep the fires burning. His two youngest daughters, both young girls, will join when their age permits.

Kent is also a kicking bass player and part of the rockabilly band, The Carpetbaggers.

Therefore, the two tattoos.

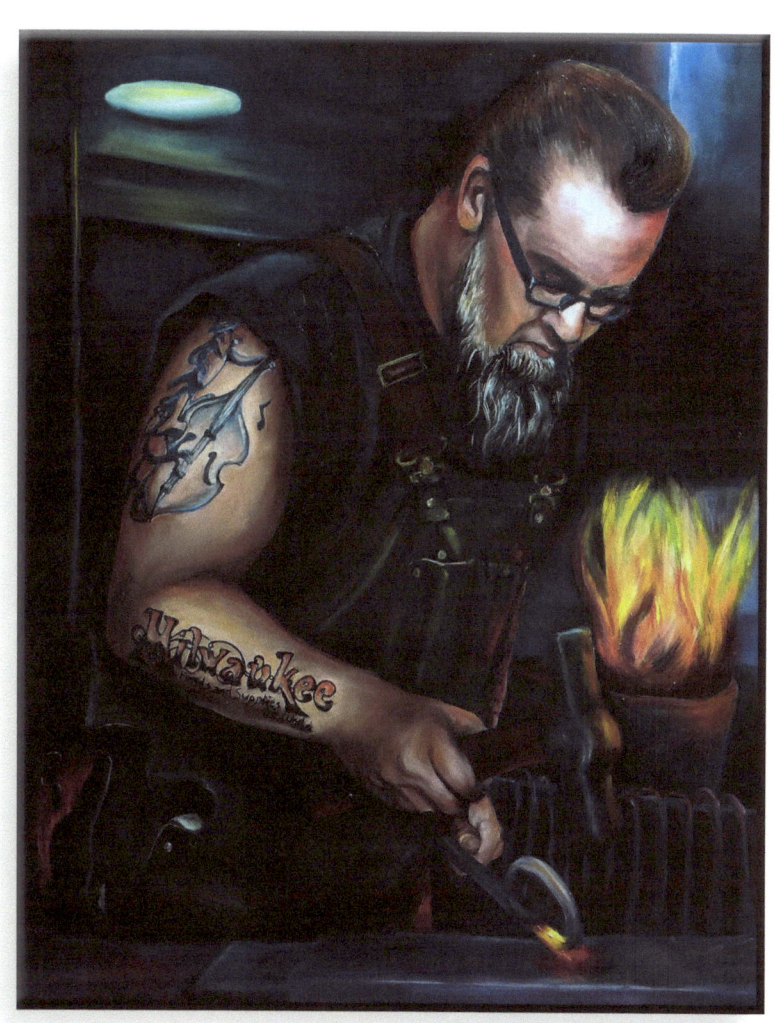

2015
Oil on panel
30" x 24"

How Philo's Brain Works

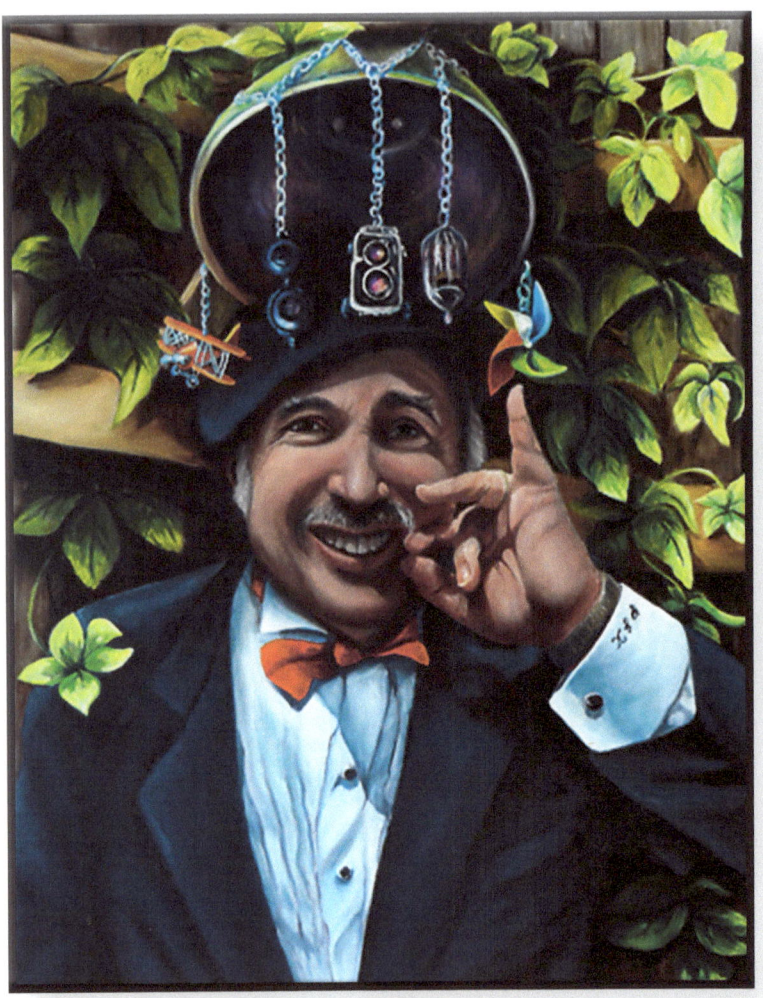

Philip "Philo" Kassner: my husband, my muse, my love, and my best friend.

His brain is a mystery to all who know him. His humor is a whirligig of puns, obscure references, and impish ideas. We all love that fact.

2015
Oil on panel
30" x 24"

Viking Soul

Mike "Ringo" White is an institution at our wonderful lake front. He can be seen walking along the beaches during our coldest of winters and hottest of summers. Ringo collects bits and pieces of colorful detritus along the shoreline and assembles them into vibrant mosaics. He is a kind and gentle soul and a man of quiet intellect.

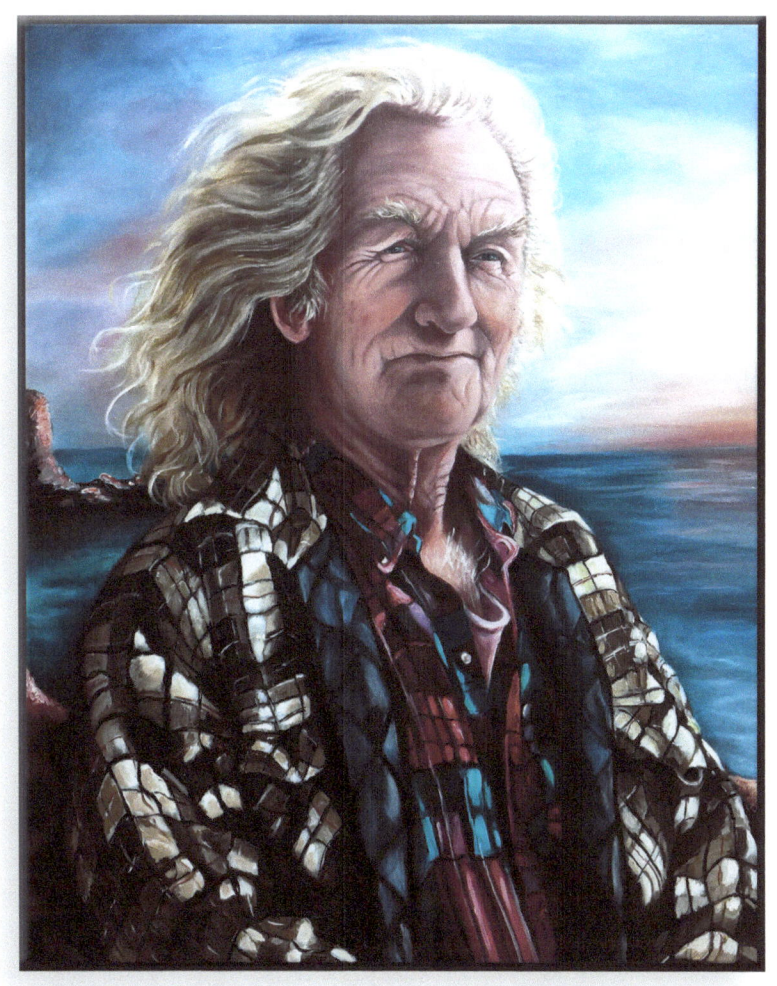

2016
Oil on panel
30" x 24"

Up from the Underground

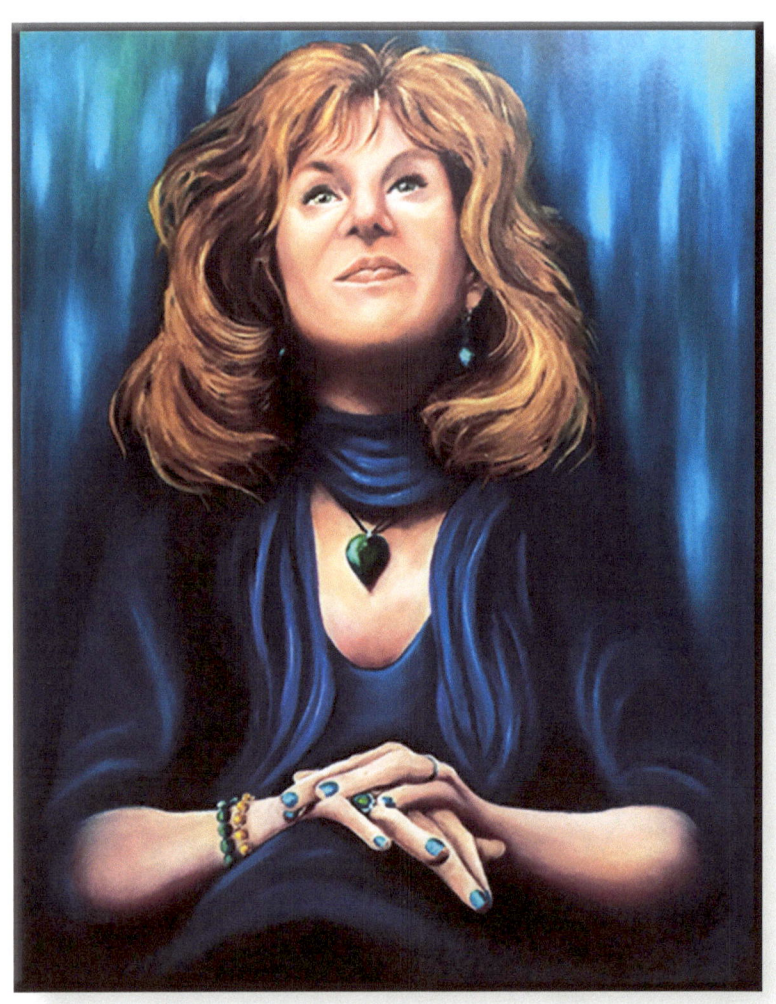

Rachel Raven is a singer/songwriter and one of the most talented entertainers I know. Her voice can wail the blues and then become a soft scintillating lullaby. She is a woman of strength, resolve, and compassion and those qualities are reflected in her music.

She was visiting one autumn and during our conversations this idea for her portrait emerged.

The title for the portrait is the title of one of her songs written when she was a busker in the Boston subways. Her voice would stop busy commuters and overcome the din and hubbub of the trains, people, and traffic.

2016
Oil on panel
30" x 24"

The Mayor Reads a Story

John Norquist was mayor of Milwaukee from 1988 to 2003. He is now living in Chicago and teaching at Loyola University. Philo had been in contact with him about another matter and jokingly asked me if I'd consider doing a portrait of the mayor. Surprisingly, he agreed.

John Norquist is a very tall man and I am a short woman. I wanted to show him with the Chicago skyline in the background but the height difference between us made for poor photos. We returned to his home. He asked us in to warm up from the February chill and offered to read us a story about his neighborhood. He grabbed the book and relaxed into his favorite chair.

I saw my opportunity.

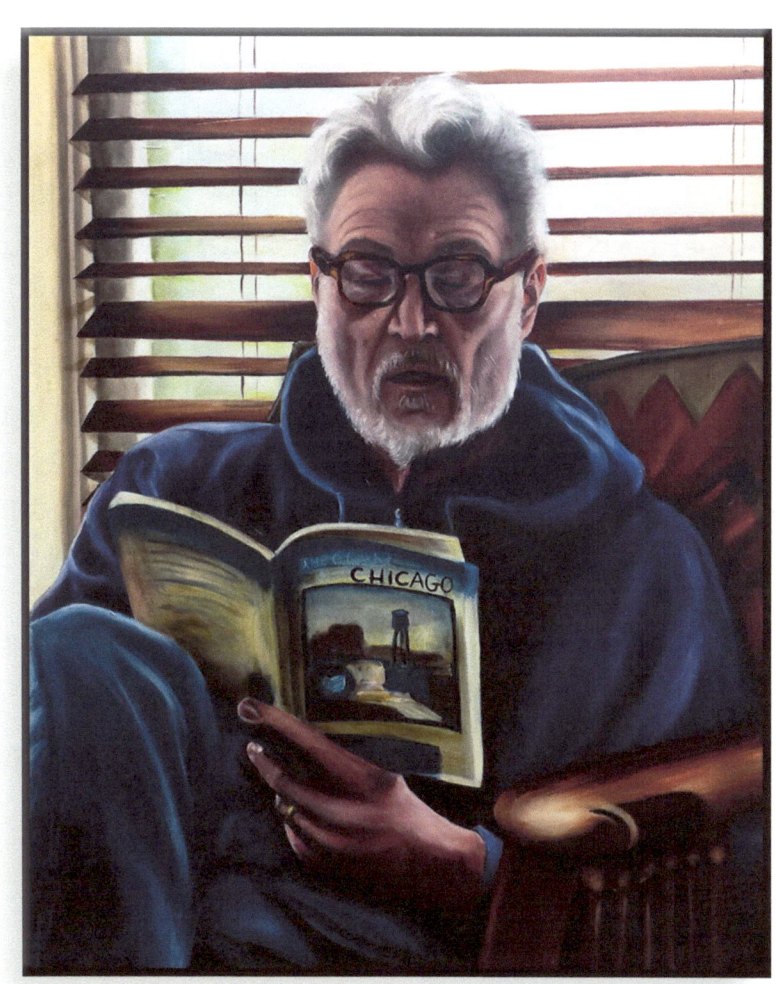

2016
Oil on panel
30" x 24"

www.ingramcontent.com/pod-product-compliance
Lightning Source LLC
Chambersburg PA
CBHW051104180526
45172CB00002B/768